Eight Miles of Muddy Road
by
Sylvia Nickels

Eight Miles of Muddy Road
by Sylvia Nickels
ISBN 1-4116-1602-2
Copyright © 2004

Online editions may also be available for this
title. For more information, please visit
http://www.Lulu.com
Lulu Enterprises, Inc.

Dedication

This book is dedicated to the memory of my parents, John Elmer and Athey Rush Maner. And to my siblings in gratitude for their encouragement for my writing. Six of them walked those muddy roads with me. My seventh living sibling, our baby sister, is a city slicker who grew up in a world of paved streets. But we love her anyway.

J. E. Maner family
Villa Rica, GA, 1956

Contents

Dedication
Introduction

                                          Page#
Persimmon Memories   1
Daddy Was a Sharecropper   11
Eight Miles of Muddy Road   17
Livin' On Alabamer Time   27
Ahead of Her Time   35
Clay Pigs Can't Squeal 39
Draketown Scholar   51
Draketown   65
Movin' Again? 71
Second Hand Easter Dress   77
Let the Games Begin   87
Sibling Support 97
Almost Our House   111
Notes 124
Columns 130

Introduction

This 'coming of age' book, as they're called now, has been churning around in my spirit for some time. The stories in it recount some of the experiences of my early years as I and my siblings trod the red dirt roads of rural Georgia in the 'forties and 'fifties.

There were plenty of cows around, but I would hardly describe Georgia, then or now, as the 'land of milk and honey.' Mamaw and Papaw Brown usually kept a cow and shared her milk with us, providing our cornbread and buttermilk suppers.

A couple of times we also kept a cow. Once when we lived in the little house that was 'almost ours' in rural Haralson County and again after we had moved to the town of Villa Rica, in Carroll County. Yes, you could still keep livestock in towns back then.

As to honey, in a corner of the Draketown School yard stood a towering tree with leafless limbs. Presumably in the spring the limbs possessed leaves, but in my long-stored memory picture, they are bare. By fall the long pods the limbs also bore were black and sticky. When split, the pods oozed a golden sweet substance like honey. Someone told me it was a locust tree.

In Sunday School I heard from the teachers about John the Baptist eating locusts and honey in the wilderness while he got instruction from God about preaching. I knew honey bees made honey, but until I attended Draketown School I didn't know that it grew on trees, so to speak, in Georgia. So I guess I can chalk that up as one more thing I learned there.

When we moved to Villa Rica I was in high school. Most of the stories in this volume hark back to earlier years. They are not in exact chronological order, but grouped roughly by subject.

Daddy was a sharecropper for many of my growing-up years, but sometimes he had a job in 'public works,' in the small towns and communities around which we lived and often moved. Before I was graduated from high school, I had attended eight schools, several of them at two or three different times.

Both my parents came from large families and so we were never far from cousins, aunts, uncles, and other extended family. Daddy and his four brothers and two sisters were orphaned when their natural parents died within weeks of each other when Daddy was six. The other children went to various unrelated families. But a cousin, Shady Elizabeth 'Mote' Brown, and her husband, Millard, took Daddy to raise as their own. They were Mamaw and Papaw to us and we were blessed to have them as grandparents. We loved to visit them, in spite of a few quirks which I've chronicled in their own chapter. No one who saw her picture would guess, but Mamaw was a woman ahead of her time with many and varied talents.

There were ups and downs in my childhood, but I don't believe I was irreparably damaged by the fact that we lived in what would now be called abject poverty. Perhaps because parents and family on both sides were never far away from us and I never doubted that we were deeply loved.

And that brings me to the reason I took pen in hand, or fingers to keyboard, and began this story several years ago. Books have been written around the stereotype of growing up in the poor, rural South. Reading them, one might think that anyone who grew up in the poverty of the pre-industrial South was of the illiterate, moonshine-swilling, worst kind of 'poor, white trash' who smoked homemade cigarettes and chewed tobacco. I'll have to grant the smoking and chewing tobacco. But most of the people I knew were of the hard-working, respectable, church-going, family oriented persuasion.

The legacy Daddy and Mother left was not houses and possessions. Those things can be acquired with a little motivation and work, as their children and grandchildren pretty well demonstrate. But what can never be acquired by striving is the feeling of security and acceptance in the bond of family in which we were raised. Perhaps, when recognized as an adult, that lack can be filled somewhat, with outside help. Even within that bond, bad events, wrong decisions, and disputes still happen. But with family undergirding lives, they are easier to overcome, I believe.

Most evidence of sharecropper life in the post-depression and pre- and post-World War II South is as 'gone with the wind' as Scarlett O'Hara's early life. Probably this is a good thing. I hope this account of one family's experience of that time will interest some readers.

Sylvia Maner Nickels
October 2004

Persimmon Memories

In my adopted state of Tennessee, the swing of the seasons is more vivid than it is further south. Late September and October in my native Georgia bring only a change from green to brown leaves. In the mountains of Tennessee, they change from the dusty green of late summer to gorgeous multi-hued patches, like a prize quilt, covering the plains and pillow hills.

Sometimes I wax nostalgic, when I hear the wail of a train, or smell the pungent odor of burning pine logs, carried through still autumn air. Memory vignettes of life experienced four hundred miles south and more than fifty years ago become as real as the house across the street.

In those halcyon days of memory, the straight, white plumes rose from every chimney through clear air into the blue sky. The frosty air carried sounds over the countryside for miles. I heard the shrill steam whistle at the sawmill near Draketown calling the men to work; the bass throb of the engine on the school bus as it strained to pull the long hill above Mill Creek; a freight train shrieking its warning at the crossing in Temple, eight miles away.

The train could be headed to Atlanta, then south to Savannah's docks on the green Atlantic, or rumbling west toward Alabama, crossing two more states and the mighty Mississippi. After rolling through Texas plains and over Rocky Mountain passes, it might continue all the way to ports on that other sea, the wide Pacific. The drawn-out lament of the steam engines of my very early years and later, of powerful diesels, stirred my imagination. I dreamed of stepping aboard the sleek passenger train they called the *Nancy Hanks*, to be spirited into the city and exciting adventures.

Instead of high adventure, my world was fields of shoulder-high cotton plants waiting to be stripped of their harvest. The bushy plants grew out of the rich, red dirt in endless rows. They drooped with open, needle-tipped bolls, or pods, filled with marshmallow-white fluff.

After the morning sun dried its dew-dampness, we filled our picksacks with the white stuff, then emptied the sacks into the big baskets spaced around the field. Crimson spots on the snowy cotton sometimes marked where the boll tips had pricked our fingers. Maybe the pods were reluctant to give up the bounty they had produced during long, hot summer days.

Some of those fields of cotton had been planted by Papaw and Mamaw. My sister, Doris, and I loved to visit their place, which was a little larger and, in our eyes, a lot more interesting than our smaller farm. They, like our Daddy, cultivated the land on shares for Uncle Davis. Not understanding such niceties of ownership, we considered it Papaw's farm.

Their house looked much larger than it was due to the long L-shaped porch. Spring and summer, the porch blazed with Mamaw's pots of crimson geraniums, orange marigolds, and petunias in every hue of the rainbow.

Enclosing part of the porch in the fall, temporary boards for half their height would be nailed to the posts supporting the roof. We emptied the baskets of cotton there each day for a week or so, before it was taken to the gin and sold.

The temptation to jump and roll on the soft, white mass, compacting the long staple cotton, was often too much for us. The grownups scolded, telling us that the packed down cotton would not bring as much money. We risked a 'switching' on our bare legs if they caught us again. We heard, but soon forgot. The sting of the switch, a supple,

4

green sprout torn from the trunk of a peach tree, reminded us.

Across the road from the house was a big, two level, tin-roofed barn, built on a slope. Two mules that pulled the heavy plow for Papaw and a milk cow shared the dark, acrid-smelling ground level. Papaw dropped the hay stored on the upper level, fragrant with sun and rain, down to them through a hole in the floor.

The birth of a lovable, awkward little calf 'freshened' the cow in the spring. The calf was sold, to our sorrow, after weaning. Mamaw pulled on the cow's teats with her strong, tanned hands, filled an enamel bucket with the sweet milk. Morning milk was added to the milk from the night before in the earthenware churn.

During the day, in the heat of the kitchen, the cream rose to the top of the milk and 'clabbered.' In early afternoon, half an hour of vigorous churning with the wooden dasher, a three foot long rod with small crossed pieces of wood attached at the bottom end, produced a couple of pounds of sweet, fresh butter. We wanted to do the churning, but small hands soon tired and we had to give the job back.

A cat, chickens, and hogs also lived on the farm. The cat would sit in perfect stillness on the edge of the hole in the barn floor. Suddenly she would launch her body with perfect accuracy toward an unwary rat. A brief, high-pitched squeal announced her usual efficient dispatch of the rat. Returning to her post, she thoroughly washed away all evidence of the execution.

We scattered corn for the chickens, and carefully collected the eggs from the nests in the shed. In the spring we had to be careful not to disturb the setting hens, clucking to themselves, patiently keeping their eggs warm. But in the fall the chicks which had hatched from those eggs were pullets and half-grown roosters. The ones who survived Sunday and holiday dinners through the winter produced their own eggs and chicks the next spring.

The fattened hogs, in ignorance of their fate, grunted and rooted for acorns in the hog pen a little way from the house. They were slaughtered early on the morning of the first hard frost. Hams and shoulders were hoisted from the rafters in the smokehouse, sausage and pickled feet were canned to provide meat for winter.

That first frost brought something besides an untimely end for the hogs. The globes on the 'simmon (persimmon) tree changed from the mouth-drawing bitterness of the green fruit to orange-red, gooey pulp. Giggling, we stood under the tree, stuffing stained mouths with the quarter-sized delicacies, rich and sweet as sugar.

Soon we gathered the nuts fallen from two tall pecan trees, competing with chattering squirrels, who took their share while we slept. We shelled the rich pecan meats into bowls before a log fire. Mamaw scolded us to leave enough for her fruit cakes and pecan pies.

At bedtime, we nestled on the soft feather bed in Mamaw's spare room, warm and cozy under her hand-pieced, patchwork quilts. The low drone of the grownups' voices lulled us to sleep. They sat, talking and rocking on the porch, under the round harvest moon that seemed caught in the branches of the huge oak tree in the yard.

The mouth-watering smell of frying bacon and Mamaw's biscuits baking in the black iron wood-fired cookstove pulled us from the deep, untroubled sleep of children. From the reservoir on the side of the stove Mamaw dipped warm water into the wash pan for us to wash hands and faces. She offered us scrambled eggs and buttered biscuits with homemade apple jelly or pear preserves, but we begged for 'soaky' - weak coffee poured over crumbled up biscuits, then sprinkled with sugar.

Following our 'soaky' breakfast, we trailed Mamaw outside as she scattered bread crumbs or corn for the chickens and slopped the hogs. Around mid-morning she would take a sausage biscuit and water in a Mason jar wrapped in a brown paper bag to Papaw, who was working in the field.

The roar of a modern-day jet on its flight path down the valley to the nearby airport jolts me back to the present. Georgia cotton fields and hand-churned butter are many adventures ago. But a poignant whiff of wood smoke carried on an autumn breeze can recreate them in an instant. And memories, like persimmons, grow sweeter with the frost of years.

Millard & Mote Brown - front
J. E. 'El' & Athey Maner

Daddy Was a Sharecropper

Mother said Daddy worked for a quarter a day when they first got married. Though only fifteen years old, which Mother did not know at the time, he was big for his age and did a man's work. He did odd jobs and day labor for local farmers and small businesses through the CCC, the Civilian Conservation Corps.

President Roosevelt and Congress had set up this government bureau to provide jobs for the thousands of unemployed men to help them support their families. The time was 1934, the country was deep in economic depression and men were glad to take any kind of job, for the most minuscule of pay.

For a year or so after they married they lived with Mamaw and Papaw, who had raised Daddy. While they were courting, she said they had their picture taken by someone with a camera at a church singing but Daddy stuck the picture in his pocket before it was dry and it was ruined. He was afraid Mamaw and Papaw would see it. Mother didn't know why he was so concerned that they not find out about their courtship and plans for marriage until after the wedding. Daddy had told her that he was seventeen, the same as her age.

Having always lived far back in the country, she was very bashful and shy. She was the oldest of, at that time, eight children, six girls and two boys. Grandma bore four other children after Mother left home. Three girls and a boy, but the boy didn't live.

My oldest sister and I are older than our three youngest aunts. This intrigued us as children, though in fact it is not too uncommon in a family with many children .

We, too, lived deep in the country until I was about twelve years old, except for a stint in a cotton mill village in Alabama. We walked the red dirt roads up to Aunt Bertha's house, and to Mamaw's, and to neighbors houses.

The nearest paved road was US Highway 78, or The Bankhead, main route going west out of Atlanta to Birmingham. It ran through Temple, the nearest country town, about eight miles away, and Bremen, a few miles further. With Draketown, they were the only towns I knew much of anything about until I was nearly twelve and we went to Atlanta to visit Daddy's sister, Aunt Margaret.

Papaw cultivated other men's land on shares, as did our grandfather on Mother's side. About the year I was born probably, when he was nineteen years old, Daddy began making a living for his own young and growing family by sharecropping, too. Mother told us about raising crops for other farmers in the area. But during the years after I grew old enough that I can remember, Daddy mostly sharecropped on the farm of one of Mother's uncles.

Sharecroppers, or tenant farmers, usually worked the land on halves with the owner, though sometimes the split was different, depending on what the tenant brought to the deal. The landowner provided a house for the sharecropper's family, the land, seed, equipment, mules to pull the plow, and the tenant the labor. At harvest time the owner got half of everything that was grown.

When I began to notice this division of the results of our labor taking place, though not old enough to have learned of the responsibilities of property ownership like taxes and upkeep, I resented Uncle Davis taking half of our peanuts and sorghum syrup. I didn't see why he should get half of the crop we had worked so hard to raise. Especially since there were so many of us and we needed it worse than he did, so I thought.

When Daddy wasn't sharecropping, and sometimes during the summer, after the crops were 'laid by', he worked at sawmills. They were dangerous places to work and Mother worried about him. The Georgia pine woods were filled with these sawmills, with their huge piles of sawdust as mute evidence of the many trees reduced to slabs of rough lumber. Some of the men lost fingers, toes, even limbs to the voracious round saws.

Cotton was still king in the south, though boll weevils had made inroads in the crops. In later years imported cotton took a further toll and now very little is grown in Georgia. Each small town seemed to boast a textile or cotton mill. Daddy worked in his share of those, also. It was hard work and long hours, but many women, including several of my aunts, made a living by working in the mills, too. Either out of necessity because they were single, through death or divorce, or to help their husbands make ends meet.

Eight Miles of Muddy Road

Not long ago my sister, Janis, emailed all her brothers and sisters, myself being the most far-flung, I guess, of her somewhat sudden plans for remarriage, giving date, location, and time - the upcoming weekend, a city park in her town, at noon on Saturday. We've played phone tag a lot, especially when both of us were working, but email always gets through. Without it, even some family members living closer to her might not have known of her impending nuptials.

The next Friday, in my fairly new car, I drove the first half of the seven hundred mile round trip to LaGrange, Georgia. Sunday evening, back home in Tennessee, I dragged through my front door, worn-out from six hours of high speed driving on smooth four-lane Interstate highways.

My mind tries to reject what memory assures me is true. Years ago when the family needed to go to town, it took almost as many hours as my Interstate jaunt to my sister's wedding. A farm wagon pulled by a pair of stalwart mules called Maud and Blackie carried us over the eight miles of red mud road from 'Johnny's little house' near Draketown, to Temple. More about that little house that I felt was 'almost ours' in a later chapter.

One trip, when I was five or six years old, stands out for me. A heavy rain had fallen the night before and the red mud, symbol of Georgia in my mind, was inches deep in places. The oozing mixture of water and fine clay soil clung to the sturdy wooden wagon wheels, stalling our forward progress at times.

18

On the steepest hill, a mile or so from our destination, Mamaw, Papaw, Mother, and Daddy left the wagon and slogged through the mud on foot to ease the load for the mules. The mules' wide eyes rolled wildly, though their field of vision was narrowed by leather blinders on either side to reduce their fear, and foam blew from their snorting lips. Daddy and Papaw swore at them and slapped the lines on their heaving flanks to urge them on.

I felt so sorry for the poor creatures as they struggled for footing, hooves slipping and powerful muscles straining. Stubborn and tough, true to their long heritage as beasts of burden, they succeeded in pulling the cumbersome wagon up that hill. I'm sure they were content to rest in their harness on the street while we enjoyed our trip to town.

Before modern paving spread to the country, Georgia roads, especially in winter, consisted of those deep ruts filled with the slick, treacherous, crimson mud. In summer the arrival of the mailman, women mail carriers were rare then, was heralded by a cloud of stifling, reddish dust while his car was still some distance away. The country folk tracked his progress as he stopped at each roadside mailbox.

Cars were not an unusual sight, but very much fewer in number and far less dependable at the time. An auto trip many times involved at least one stop to mend a blown-out tire. New tires were scarce during World War Two and the years immediately after, as the military required most of the tire rubber available.

When we needed to go to town or visit a neighbor, we most often walked or rode in the farm wagon. This mode of transportation gave us a closer relationship to roads, especially our usually bare feet, than most of us have now.

After heavy rains, we knew which roads were impassable because the babbling brooks they crossed had become raging torrents with no bridges. We knew which road would be smoother for a time because the county highway department had 'scraped.' it.

A heavy grader, a wide, angled steel blade on the front, would scrape and smooth out the ruts. Then dump trucks would spread a layer of crushed rock on the more level surface. The improved roadway was easier on car transmissions, but painful for bare feet.

A few years after the woeful mule-drawn wagon trip to Temple, when we had moved to a house on Hwy. 101 out of Villa Rica, Mother roused us children very early, before daylight. We piled in our old Chevrolet, which was in much better shape than the jalopies Daddy drove up to that time, to go and visit Daddy's youngest sister, Aunt Margaret, and her family in Atlanta. I thought of that city as being unimaginably far away, though it was actually only about forty miles by The Bankhead, as the highway was called.

US Highway 78, The Bankhead, was the nearest paved road in our county and passed through Temple. The modern concrete highway was named for Alabama's U. S. Senator Bankhead, one of the early proponents of what has become the Federal Highway System.

Six miles west of Temple The Bankhead continued through a somewhat larger town named Bremen. These were the only two towns with which I was actually familiar as a child, though I knew of the existence of others. I heard the grownups speak of visiting Dallas, Rockmart, Cedartown, and Tallapoosa, other small Georgia towns. I understood that The Bankhead continued on past Bremen and Tallapoosa to the Alabama town named Oxford, near which we actually lived for nearly a year when I was in third grade, then Heflin, and, in the misty distance, Birmingham. Altogether the world as I knew it had a radius of perhaps a hundred miles until I was nearly in my 'teens.

My reading textbooks, which I devoured early in each school term, showed me a much larger world of big cities full of factories and tall buildings filled with sets of rooms called apartments, but it seemed unreal. I longed to experience that world, but wondered if I ever would.

Sometimes when someone in my own family is ill and bills pile up, I'd like to return to that smaller, simpler world of muddy roads. But many of the tiny towns of my youth have been consumed by Metro Atlanta. Only in memory can I walk to Mamaw's or Aunt Bertha's along those unpaved roads, for few of them remain either. Most are paved and many rerouted past recognition.

At least, the majority of roads in and around the mid-section of the state are paved. I have discovered that many unpaved roads remain in south Georgia. David Royer of the Brunswick, Georgia News reported around the time of this writing that Brantley County has the lowest percentage of paved roads in Georgia, about one-third. And when severe weather, such as the inches of rain from this year's hurricanes, comes through, Brantley and other south Georgia residents still have many transportation problems.

So I'll celebrate the present smooth blacktop rather than eight miles of muddy road between Draketown and Temple. And not attempt a nostalgic country tune along the lines of the venerable Grandpa Jones' *Eight More Miles to Louisville*.

In today's world I'm connected to friends and loved ones in a way far beyond my childhood comprehension. Instead of a cloud of rosy dust announcing its arrival, a diminutive mailbox with a tiny red flag pops up on my computer screen and an animated voice announces, "You've got mail."

Millard and Mote Brown

Livin' on 'Alabamer' Time

A popular country song recorded a few years ago by Don Williams was *Livin' on Tulsa Time*. The underlying idea was apparently that the singer lived by a different time than his surroundings. My Mamaw and Papaw managed that feat long before Don sang about it.

They lived in rural Haralson County, Georgia, which was (and is) in the Eastern Standard Time zone. But they kept their clocks set on 'Alabamer' time, as we called Central Standard Time. After Daylight Savings Time was introduced, their clocks were right at least half the year, since they would never 'spring forward' or 'fall back.' Why they chose to live on Central Standard Time is a mystery, at least to me. If Daddy knew the reason, he kept it to himself.

Mamaw and Papaw never lived in neighboring Alabama, or even visited that state, as well as I remember. Though my father moved us there, three times, during my childhood. Daddy was their only son. Possibly they felt closer to him and us grandchildren if their clocks matched ours and that's when they started keeping their clocks set an hour slower than the prevailing time in Haralson County. Such sentimentality seems a little out of character for a hard-working couple who farmed most of their lives, rooted and grounded in Georgia's rich, red dirt. But loving grandparents that they were, it's possible.

Or maybe being out of step, time-wise, was a way of declaring their unity in overcoming the shadow of illegitimacy under which they'd both grown up, a heavy burden in those days. This bond would probably have been unspoken by such a strong, reclusive couple, but I can believe it.

Mamaw's mother lived with them from the time I can remember. Aunt Frone was actually our Great Aunt, as she was sister to my Daddy's natural father. She was the widow of a much older man, though he was not Mamaw's father. We never knew the identity of that mysterious person.

The fact that Mamaw and Papaw were illegitimate was not a family secret. But it was rarely spoken about. Naturally, our curiosity was aroused by a subject the grownups preferred not to discuss. As children we pestered Daddy and Mother with questions all we dared, but to no avail.

I had married and moved to Tennessee before Mamaw and Papaw grew too old to farm and Daddy moved them into town. I'm sure they continued their custom and died a few years later, as they had lived, on 'Alabamer' time.

Both while they lived and after their deaths, our Mamaw and Papaw were favorite subjects of our conversations. Below I recount my youngest brother's recollections of a story about ball lightning that Papaw told him at some point. I remember the episode, as I was nine so Ray would have been about three.

Millard Brown could tell some whoppers when it came to telling stories. Since I was only a young boy I didn't know if they were true or not. My upbringing was to believe what adults told me but especially if that adult was Mother, Daddy, Mawmaw, or Pawpaw. Since this was Pawpaw telling this story I can only assume that it was true. He went on to tell, "It was the late afternoon after a hot day. The sky got dark, the wind started blowing, and flashes of lightning began to streak across the sky. Loud claps of thunder made the walls shake." His story started sounding scary to me so I eased over closer to my dad. "Just then a lightning bolt struck the house", he went on to say. "Right after that the light bulb hanging down from the ceiling just got so bright and busted into a thousand pieces.

From the socket where the light bulb use to be a big ball of fire fell down to some inches above the floor."

He indicated that everyone scrambled back against the walls to get out of the way. "As we watched that ball of lightning floating across the room we could hear it sizzling like electricity. As it floated more in one direction you could tell it was headed for the fireplace." Now everybody knew that a fireplace has a chimney and that the chimney creates a draft of air that can suck a piece of burning ember right up it. "So we were all hoping that ball lightning would just go right on up that chimney and out of there, which is exactly what it did. Just as soon as that ball got close to that fireplace opening, swoosh! Up it turned and quicker than it appeared, it was gone."

"ENCYCLOPÆDIA BRITANNICA Ball lightning also called Globe Lightning, aerial phenomenon that occurs as a moving luminous sphere several inches in diameter. It usually occurs near the ground during thunderstorms, may be red, orange, or yellow in colour, and is often accompanied by a hissing sound and distinct odour.

It lasts only a few seconds and dies out suddenly, either silently or explosively. Ball lightning has been observed to cause damage by burning or melting. Its relation, if any, to common lightning is uncertain. Its causes are unknown, but among the explanations of ball lightning are the following: air or gas behaving abnormally; high-density plasma; an air vortex containing luminous gases; and microwave radiation within a plasma shell. Information about this topic in other articles: ball lightning, plasmas, The lower atmosphere and surface of the Earth from plasma. - Index Entry ball lightning - Internet Links."

Ray has other stories about Papaw and other family members on his website, http://www.raymaner.com, well worth a visit.

As I recall, there were two different incidents of ball lightning in the house in question, which was 'Johnny's big house.' One happened pretty much as Papaw recounted it to Ray. The other episode was a little different. There was an electrical outlet, we called them 'plug ins,' about head high (my head, anyway) on the wall between the kitchen and living room.

During another severe thunderstorm electricity, or lightning, jumped from the electrical outlet and 'whooshed' toward the fireplace. All of us were in the room, seated in chairs, on the floor, or on one of the beds. At the time, neither we or Mamaw and Papaw had a living room with just couch and chairs. Fortunately no one was in the direct path of the lightning, which looked like a globe of fire, four or five inches in diameter.

I think the lightning striking and coming into the house surprised us as it had grounded lightning rods mounted on both gables of the roof. Most times in those days houses did not have the rods and usually burned down when lightning struck.

Ahead of Her Time

As I mentioned in my Introduction, Mamaw was a woman ahead of her time, with many talents. She was a strong woman, physically and mentally. I think Daddy married Mother because he unconsciously recognized that she also would be a strong woman. He probably realized before too long, as do many hapless men, that being bound to two strong women is not the most peaceful place to find oneself.

No doubt Mamaw and Papaw knew that Daddy was too young to marry. But at fifteen, he was strong-willed. They would support the marriage or he was gone. I'm sure they dropped their opposition in order to give the marriage a chance to succeed. Which it did, pretty well, for thirty-seven years.

I can remember Mamaw laboring side-by-side with Papaw in the fields. Then she did the milking, cooking, vegetable gardening, canning and preserving, as well as keeping a very clean house.

Mamaw made a piece of furniture for the newlyweds which always stood in Mother and Daddy's bedroom. A wooden cabinet, three or four feet high, we called it a washstand. But the lower section, behind two doors, actually always held the younger children's clean clothing. I believe there were two small drawers above the doors. I wish I had persuaded my husband that we take it when we siblings were deciding what to do with her things after Mother's death.

I do possess a bit of Mamaw's handiwork, though. She made a rolling pin for Mother from a piece of wood about eighteen inches long. By some means, she cut part of it out on either end so the remaining wood formed two inch handles. Then she used a piece of broken glass and tediously scraped it until the whole thing was very smooth.

I regret not being close enough to know Mamaw well after I was old enough to appreciate her. By the time I was thirteen and in high school, we were living in Villa Rica. Mamaw and Papaw were still in the country in Haralson County and I didn't see them as often. Then came graduation, I moved to Atlanta to work.

After I married, I saw them a few times, in the country and after Daddy moved them to Villa Rica also. While I was pregnant with my daughter, Papaw was hospitalized for serious surgery, the first time he'd ever been in the hospital. When my daughter was three months old, we moved to Tennessee and I don't recall seeing them again.

Clay Pigs Can't Squeal

With chubby six year old fingers, I reached out to touch one of the brown and black pigs Mother had modeled out of the brown mud and red clay in our yard. We lived near Corinth Church at the time, about five miles from 'Johnny's little house.'

From curly tail made of twisted string to its flat-nosed snout, it looked just like the porker on Papaw's farm, always dirty from rolling in the sticky, black mud of the pigpen. The pig, actually a good-sized hog, squealed and splashed through the mud to the feed trough when it saw Mamaw coming with the slopbucket filled with used dishwater and table scraps.

Mother possessed genuine creative talent. But the drudgery of cooking, cleaning, and caring for five children under ten, baby Jack only two months old, left her little time to enjoy her gift. And with so many mouths to feed, art supplies were out of the question.

Her usual creative outlet was to put beauty into the practical things she made for us. Like the pieced quilts, some with intricate designs, which kept us warm in winter. Baby clothes and pillowcases bore touches of embroidery, as did doilies and table runners. And with needle and thread, lacking even a treadle sewing machine, she cut apart and remade our charity box clothes so they fitted as though bought for us.

I don't know where she got the idea of sculpting the pigs. Maybe from watching us kids make mud pies. Her paints were of the simplest sort, I'm sure. They might have been charcoal

40

pulled from the ashes in the wood-fired cookstove and crushed berries or tree bark.

Mother had strictly ordered us to stay away from the clay pigs. I knew I wasn't supposed to touch them. But I was fascinated by how real they appeared. I was and am a tactile person, always needing to explore any object by touching, patting, rubbing. I didn't see how it could hurt anything to pick one up for just a second to get a better look.

I couldn't know that the clay and sand Mother had used made a fragile sculpting medium, especially while still damp. To my dismay, the pig broke right in two. No one else was in the room so I quickly put it back down, trying, unsuccessfully, to stick the halves back together.

Since we lived next door to a church, Doris and I went to Sunday School. Mother and Daddy were 'good people', loved their children, and attended church sometimes. The whole family would enjoy all day singings with preaching and 'dinner on the grounds.' I knew the right thing to do was to go to Mother and admit my guilt.

But I was afraid. When Mother was mad about something, she seemed a different person. Not the loving mother who rocked all night before the fire place, crooning to soothe Baby Jack's earache. I hurried outside and was playing with the others when Mother discovered the broken pig.

She called us into the house - Doris, two years older than me; Margaret, four years old; and John, almost two. Her voice was tight and full of anger. "Which one of you broke the pig I molded? After I told you not to even touch them!"

"Not me!"

"I didn't."

We all denied the deed, either in words or by exchanging blank looks.

"Which one?" She demanded, voice shrill and incensed.

Mother's eyes were narrowed and fierce-looking. I knew I should admit that I was the guilty one, but I could not. My heart beat fast and my mouth was dry. I absolutely could not speak thc words that would direct her anger solely toward me.

We stood before her, fidgeting and twisting our clothes. Finally, when it became apparent to her that none of us was going to own up to the crime, she decided on a course of action.

"Doris, Sylvie, you're both old enough that you knew better." I felt relief at her words, even as they added to my guilt.

"Margaret, John, come out here in the yard." She ordered angrily.

The younger children looked frightened. Doris and I exchanged puzzled looks. What was she going to do to them? Wc followed along behind them.

Mother walked over to one of the bushes in the yard. She marked out a circle in the sand. "Sit there!" She ordered the by now crying youngsters. "And don't either one of you move until you tell me the truth."

And there the blameless children sat through the long afternoon plaintively weeping and protesting their innocence while my guilt gnawed at me. Finally she let them move from their circle prison. We were all very subdued the rest of the day and did not argue when sent to bed at our usual early hour.

I don't remember whatever happened to the clay pigs or if Mother was able to repair the broken one. As I recall, it was her only venture into sculpting. But through the years and in spite of having several more children, she continued to try to bring a measure of softness and beauty into our drab lives.

The beds of petunias, zinnias, and geraniums always in the yards of our rented homes are now only bright spots in our fond recollections of a remarkable woman. But several of the cozy quilts her nimble fingers created and the landscapes she painted in her later years now grace my home.

Only years later, after we were all grown up, did I have the courage to admit that I was the guilty party that day and asked my siblings' pardon. It had lain like a rock on my conscience for so long I was amazed that they did not remember the incident.

I now know that at six I was too young to be fully accountable for my cowardice. My only show of courage up to then had been stepping out into the darkness one night and closing our back door for a few minutes to prove I wasn't afraid of the dark. Darkness was nothing compared to Mother's anger, I felt. Even so, I do not like my younger self much when I remember that I kept silence and let my little sister and brother be punished for something I did. But maybe as the saying goes these days, 'what goes around comes around,' even at six years old.

Doris, in fourth grade, and I walked the short distance to our country school with several other kids. I, having started school at five and skipped a grade, was a fearful, tongue-tied third grader.

A little while after the broken pig incident an older boy harassed me as we walked to school. I cried and next day someone told the teacher.

Afraid of being paddled, I guess, he lied about me. He claimed that as we walked home the day before, I had called him a profane name, which he didn't take off anybody. She insisted that I apologize. Timid and frightened of her, I could not speak, to deny or apologize. Other students knew the truth, but, fearing reprisal, didn't speak up. Being my sister, Doris didn't count as a reliable witness.

A few years passed and during a revival at a little Methodist church when I was eleven, to the strains of "Just As I Am", I walked down the aisle to accept Jesus. I didn't understand it all completely, but that night my young heart was more at peace than it had been since the pig episode. I knew God had forgiven me. I wasn't so sure Mother would, so I never told her.

Doris missed too many days of school in fourth grade, due to contracting measles, so we wound up in the same grade. When we reached high school, she and I began ninth grade at

Buchanan, but finished the term at Douglas County High School. Largest school of the many we had attended, it was scary, but we had each other.

That year, during a Baptist Church revival, Mother found salvation. Afterward, with great enthusiasm, she made sure that we all attended church, twice on Sunday, on Wednesday nights, and Bible School in summer.

I learned that Bible characters weren't always brave. Even Moses ran away when God called him to lead the Hebrew children. But later he thundered to Pharaoh, "Let my people go!" And he did.

We moved again, to Villa Rica, where at last the family took root. Doris dropped out of school to take a job in a factory in Bremen. Most of her earnings went to help support the family, to the benefit of her younger siblings. The oldest of the children in school, I was now thirteen. Margaret, John, Jack and I caught the big yellow bus in front of our house. Among the kids already on the bus when it picked us up were a couple of unruly boys, who were always picking on some hapless child or other. Now they chose us.

"Look! Pharaoh's army." They taunted, pushing and shoving my little brothers . Why did they choose that phrase? We were not like wicked Pharaoh's army, but rather more like the Hebrew children wandering in the wilderness, as we'd roamed over much of west Georgia and eastern Alabama. God saved the Hebrew children. He would protect us. I charged the boys, shouting, "Leave my brothers alone!" And they did.

Sylvia Maner Nickels

Draketown Scholar

I received the greater part of my elementary education in Georgia, mostly Haralson County, but my first scholastic adventure was in Heflin, Alabama. Five years old, I'd celebrated my January birthday while we still lived in Georgia before our family moved to Alabama in early spring. My sister, Doris, two years older but a shy child, resisted new experiences. After our move, however, she had no option but to transfer to and finish first grade at Heflin Elementary.

In the fall, she was even more reluctant to return to school. So Mother fudged a little on my birth year and enrolled me in first grade so that Doris would have someone with her. Alabama law at that time, and maybe still, required that before she could start school in the fall, a child must turn six before the end of the calendar year.

I was small, even for five years, but if the school authorities marked it, they apparently said nothing. Considering the many tears I cried that year, the law was probably a good one. Even so there seems to be no permanent damage to my psyche, though some of my siblings might disagree.

Mother liked to relate one morning's incident when I felt the need to empty my bladder just as our school bus came into sight.

"Hurry, Sylvie. The bus is coming." Doris urged me to finish.

I'd gone behind a scuppernong vine to do my business, as no neighbor house was within sight on that side.

"It's all right, Doris. We'll get on the bus." I said, pulling up my little homemade panties.

Considering other events of that year, no doubt my presence was a mixed blessing for my older sister.

A certain school field trip that fall stands out for me and I've written about it elsewhere. But the most memorable experience of my first year in the world of education did not occur at Heflin. That episode happened at Draketown School, a couple of months later, after Daddy moved us back to Georgia.

The fairly new brick school building at Heflin had running water and inside restrooms. Draketown School still had wooden outhouses. The girls' toilet stood about fifty feet away, on the west side of the building and the boys' toilet the same distance on the east side.

The girls' sanitary facility, though I'm reluctant to call it that, was a rather ramshackle old structure. With no inside lighting or windows, the only illumination came through the large, sagging door and the wide cracks where the walls joined the tin roof. This toilet was a six seater, with the three nearest the door raised a couple of feet off the floor and the other three lower for the benefit of younger children.

To my still five-year-old eyes, the toilet was huge. The section with the lower seats had little illumination when the door was open, and when the door was closed, that area was quite dark. I was afraid of that toilet, with the door closed, even when other girls were inside with me.

One day during class, I felt nature's call and asked to be excused. Classes were in session and no one was about, so I decided to leave the door open and climbed up to one of the seats in front of it. Very soon, Doris came flying down the path, yelling at me. Someone had looked out from one of the classroom windows on that side of the building and informed my sister of my shameful conduct.

The school building was a square, two-story brick structure with numerous tall windows and a bell tower. Four large classrooms, two on either side of a wide hall were on the lower level. The hall led to an arched entry with a rather impressive stairway to the second floor auditorium. In that auditorium I made my first and last ever appearance on the boards in a Christmas play debut as the angel warning the wise men to go home another way.

By the second time Doris and I returned to Draketown as students, in fourth grade, a long, low frame building had been constructed behind the brick main building. It housed first, second, and third grades, as well as home ec classes for seventh grade girls.

The school grounds were surely not as extensive as the memory in my mind. But there was a fairly large red dirt baseball field just across the school yard from the main building. Adjacent to the ball field was the main driveway from the unpaved country road about fifty feet in front of the school. On the other side of the driveway was a tree-lined grassy area where we hid Easter eggs, played games, ate lunches, or generally hung out during recess.

From the road another entry to the school grounds formed the other side of the play area. This drive was rough and rutted, rarely used, and in the corner formed by it and the road grew a locust tree. The long curved black pods on the tree, when broken open, contained a sweet, honey-like substance. Having heard preachers talk about John the Baptist, thousands of years ago, eating locusts and honey in the wilderness, I wondered if they referred to these pods, still miraculously growing in Draketown, Georgia.

During my first experience at Draketown School, in first grade, my main use of the grassy area between the drives was to sit and cry. Every day. When someone asked why I was crying, I did not know. Maybe it was the stress of our move from Alabama and changing schools, in addition to my tender age. I cried some at the Alabama school, but not every day.

Apparently, crying had no adverse affect on my ability to learn. Mrs. Singleton, long-time first grade teacher at Draketown, promoted me to second grade during the last three weeks of the term. So the next fall, I entered third grade, still just six years old.

I didn't finish the third grade at Draketown though. We moved to Alabama again, this time near Oxford, when Daddy went to work at the Southern Textile Mill. We lived in the mill village and attended Oxford Elementary. Doris was in fourth grade, but she contracted red measles that year and missed a lot of school. The measles, as was said in those days, 'settled in her eyes' and she had to start wearing glasses. The teachers decided, due to her extended absence near the beginning of the year, to put her back in third grade with me. I doubt this pleased her as much as it did me.

We didn't finish third grade at Oxford, either. By the following spring, 1946, my family was back in Georgia, again in Haralson County, but not in the Draketown school district. We were enrolled at Union School, which the county closed after that year. The school, which included first through fifth grade, occupied the two downstairs rooms of a big rectangular white building. The teachers, a married couple, had living quarters upstairs. Probably twenty-five or thirty children from the surrounding farms made up the student body. I don't believe either of the teachers liked children. Or maybe they knew this was their last year at the school and they weren't happy about it.

An older boy lied to the teacher about me, saying I called him a profane name, and she tried to force me to apologize to him. Other children knew the truth, but didn't defend me. Just retribution, perhaps, as it followed my ethical lapse in the clay pigs incident.

My first experience with smoking, though officially forbidden, occurred at Union School. Rabbit tobacco grew as a wild, grayish looking plant. It somewhat resembled, as I recall, the cultivated garden plant Dusty Miller. When dried and crumbled, it had long enjoyed the status of substitute tobacco for boys unable to procure the real thing. Two or three of the older kids brought thin cigarette rolling papers and imitation tobacco to school. These materials had to be hidden in the moss in a nearby pine thicket and surreptitiously used. Being among the younger children, I got little taste of the taboo substance, which was certainly just as well.

During the following summer, adults in the community were considerably agitated. In rural areas, schools had always been closed for a few weeks in spring and fall so that children could help plant crops, mostly cotton, and harvest it.

Then Georgia passed its first compulsory school attendance law. No longer could parents legally keep their children at home at will to help with crops or during family illnesses. My father felt the state was overstepping its bounds in a big way to tell him he must send his children to school when he needed them at home. Actually, he and mother were conscientious about sending us to school, it was just the idea of the state telling him he had to do so or go to jail that galled him. The state prevailed, of course, and compulsory school attendance has come to be accepted, even in Georgia.

In the fall of 1946, Doris and I began fourth grade at Draketown School, in Miss Bess's class. By a stroke of luck, we also finished fourth grade there. During that year, I became a victim of a freak accident.

At Draketown, and maybe other schools in the area, the boys came up with a fad. Those were the days of the original classic shaped six ounce Coke bottles. These bottles were molded with a glass ring at the top, which was thicker than the body of the bottle. By some means, the boys would remove, intact, this glass circle. Then they wore these circles on their fingers like rings. Having missed a lot of school to help on family farms, and not terribly interested in school anyway, some of these strapping country boys were fifteen, sixteen years old and still in 6th or 7th grade. Not quite eight years old, somewhat small for my age, they towered over me.

As I darted along the central hallway one day, in and out of a group of boys, I felt a sharp pain on my nose. Suddenly I was covered with blood. The glass ring on the finger of one of the boys had swiped the bridge of my nose, laying it open. It probably frightened him as much as me. A teacher took me to Doctor Eaves' house/office, and he bandaged my nose. Then the teacher took me home. I was quite the little heroine for a couple of weeks, until my nose healed up. In a certain light, the scar is still visible, over fifty years later.

I came into a sizable amount of money that year. A whopping fifty cents. It was the most money I had ever possessed at one time. When we had the school Easter Egg hunt, I found the prize egg which contained two shiny quarters.

During recess we were permitted to walk to the two stores in town, a quarter mile at most from school, if we had a reason. I immediately took my windfall to town and squandered it. I lost some of it and the rest went for candy. When the candy was eaten, I was just as penniless as before. I can still remember the disappointment of having nothing to show for all that money.

Like 'Johnny's little house,' the repository of knowledge for children in and around Draketown is no more. During the 'sixties, the two story brick building had deteriorated so much it was demolished and a one level brick building erected. Finally even that was shut down and all county students bussed to Buchanan. The new building was left standing, and has housed at various times a mobile home repair shop, a flea market and appliance repair/junk shop. Now abandoned, surrounded by a couple acres of weeds, it is merely a sad eyesore to passers-by on Route 120, between Buchanan and Dallas.

Along with the fact that honey grew on trees, I learned other things while we lived around

Draketown. For a few years Mamaw and Papaw sharecropped some farm land along Highway 113 about halfway between Draketown and Temple, near District Line Church.

Four mimosa trees stood in the front yard of the little farm house where they lived. I would stand in the fine white sand under their branches and inhale the sweet smell of the lacy, pink blossoms. The house still stands, though the highway has been paved and widened through the years, taking the mimosa trees and most of the front yard.

A tub that had filled with rain water, caught for washing clothes, I suppose, sat beside the house one day when we were visiting Mamaw. Her cat had a litter and the kittens were maybe six or eight weeks old. One of the kittens either fell in the tub of water or one of us children threw it in. At any rate, to my surprise, it swam furiously to the side of the tub and climbed out. I hadn't known that kittens could swim without anyone ever teaching them how.

Draketown

Draketown, Georgia is the original 'little town
that time forgot'. From the slightly bigger town of
Temple, State Route 113 meandered through the
pint-sized metropolis for one block as its main
street before joining State Route 120 and
continuing north.

Draketown was a tiny town when I was
growing up, in the 'forties and 'fifties, and is still
smaller now, as to retail commerce. Then again,
maybe not. Two convenience food stores, which
also sell gasoline, and a small restaurant serve the
same functions as the three businesses the town

boasted then. Just up the road a mile or so there is even a bar/restaurant for the more adventurous.

Even then, Draketown was deserving of being called a town. Three general merchandise stores, which sold everything from fresh eggs to dress material, flourished on its single block. Mr. Ike's Store held down one end of the block. Reeves's Store stood at the other end, with the Reeves's residence and Stevens's Store, which housed the Oddfellows Hall on the second floor, between them.

Mr. Ike's store was full of all kinds of wonderful junk, the country version of the five and dime store in larger towns. Or our Dollar Stores today. The building burned down and Mr. Ike moved his store to a large two-story former residence on the other end of town, across from Reeves' Store, all of a hundred yards probably from his original location.

Reeves' Store had an old-fashioned round gas pump, about seven feet high, the only one in town. The reddish gas it dispensed was visible, as the top two feet or so of the pump was made of glass.

A white marble monument about twelve feet tall stood across the street from Reeves's Store. The legend on its base announced that it honored a woman killed by the bootleggers. I don't recall ever hearing the full story of the monument, or the circumstances of the woman's death.

Draketown Elementary School, Doctor Eaves' office, in his home, Draketown Baptist Church, and a few frame residences completed the town which was surrounded on all sides by farmland.

Reeves' Store, the one with a gas pump, was owned and operated by John Reeves and his wife, later by their son, John, Jr. They sold groceries and other necessities of country life, as well as gas. In the front of their store stood a big chest type floor cooler, which held racks of Coca Colas, RCs, and Orange and Grape Nehis. The top could be raised up so customers could help themselves to their choice of ice cold drinks. Such things were a special and rare treat for my siblings and me.

Doctor Eaves died, the elementary school was consolidated to the county seat, and one by one the old stores closed. Young John built a new store, also with gas pumps, over on State Highway 120. After the elder Reeves had died and my own parents were divorced, Mother stayed with the widowed Mrs. Reeves as a sort of companion for several months.

Bypassing the town, Route 113 has been paved and relocated three hundred yards or so north of where the town proper was located fifty years ago. At the new intersection it still joins Route 120, to run north as far as Rose's Crossroads where it turns west.

Just up from the 'new' store is a restaurant called The Hutch House, which has changed ownership several times in the twenty years or so of its existence. The more recent notoriety of the town is that in the restaurant parking lot one morning several years ago a young man was found shot to death in his car. The county sheriff's department soon apprehended his murderer as many knew there was bad blood between them.

No doubt other tragedies have occurred in this small place through the years. And more will likely take place, as the growing tide of refugees from the big city of Atlanta fill the area with new contemporary homes, prosperity, and the usual concerns of a more urban population.

A while back I drove along the old town street once more. Reeves's store building is falling down, the other two already gone. Full grown oak trees stand in the burnt out shell of Mr. Ike's first store site. But the marble monument to a woman's untimely death remains as does the Baptist church, larger and freshly painted.

Time may have forgotten and almost erased the little town, but it will live on in the memory of those like me who do remember it.

Moving Again?

I have only faint memories of the first time we moved to the state of Alabama. When we moved there, near a place called Blue Springs, I must have been between three and four years old. We lived in a tiny rental house owned by a man named Foshee, I think, near where Mother's parents lived at the time.

I dimly recall walking to the doctor's office with Mother when I had 'a case of dysentery,' as Mother called it. His office was in his home, not far from our house. I remember having to squat on the side of the country road before we got to the doctor's house. Fortunately, there was very little traffic in those days.

Another memory of that period is of all of us standing out in Grandma's yard, looking up at the sky. An airplane, an unusual sight at the time, was flying overhead. This would have been about 1942. I nearly backed into a team of mules hitched to a wagon waiting in the yard to go to work in the fields. Mules are not as skittish as horses, but heir hooves are just as hard. Had one connected with my small body, I would probably have flown across the yard almost as fast as the plane. Grandma ran and grabbed me up and spanked my bottom for not watching where I was going. I couldn't understand why she spanked me if she was so scared for me.

Grandma was probably quite pregnant at the time with Madge, her last child and one of my three aunts who are younger than me. When the time came for her to be born, my mother went over to help. All of us kids were sent to the farthest part of the house. I had no idea what was going on, only that in the morning there was a new baby in the bed with Grandma.

The Christmas following the birth of my newest little Aunt was a great disappointment for me. After dark on Christmas Eve, again at Grandma's house, Daddy donned Mother's red jacket and played Santa Claus. We screamed and giggled and pretended to believe it was Santa. No doubt I did believe it. The older girls received baby dolls. So did I, only mine was a little tiny plastic job, with just a diaper while their dolls were larger and had clothes. I was not happy and showed it, Mother told me, by flinging the unsatisfactory gift under a bed. But that was the breaks, and I had to play with my doll or not at all.

The airplane and doll episodes occurred during our first sojourn in Alabama. Grandpa Rush had decided to move his family from the Corinth Community to Alabama after Mother married and they remained there for most of the rest of their lives.

Later, after returning to Georgia for a couple of years, Daddy again moved us to Alabama. He had been hired at the Southern Textile Mill, near Oxford, and we lived in the mill village. We occupied half of a two family house, as were all of the houses, before such housing was called duplexes. The grown daughter of the family in the other side of our house evidently was not happy to have a family with five children next door. She would throw screaming temper tantrums and Mother, thinking she was a little crazy, cautioned us to stay away from her.

Mother's younger sister, Jewell, with her husband, Lloyd, lived in the same mill village, as did one of her two brothers, Curtis, and his wife, Winnell. Their mother, my grandmother, was visiting them all, with her four youngest daughters, among them, Patsy, a couple of years younger than me. Patsy was with us when we ate lunch one day and there were tomatoes on the table. We thought it was funny when Patsy, a farm child herself, asking for some tomato, told Mother she wanted that red potato.

While we lived in the mill village, Mother took a correspondence course to learn how to tint black and white photographs with oil paints. Color photo film was unheard of and this was the poor man's version of an oil portrait, I suppose. She enjoyed the work, though finding the time must have been a challenge for her.

This village was the nearest to town living we had ever known and we liked it. A grocery store was only a couple of blocks away, and Mother would send us to buy boxes of corn flakes and other goodies we had seldom enjoyed.

Oddly, I sprained the same arm, my left, three times during that year. The village street was gravel and I guess I wasn't accustomed to a surface that shifted and rolled under my running feet. I hadn't done much running on the gravel during a field trip in first grade a couple of years earlier, also in Alabama.

Daddy must have quit the job at the mill, probably over some minor dispute with the foreman, as he was prone to do. So by the time school started in 1947, we were back in Georgia and Doris and I were once again at Draketown School, in fourth grade.

Second-Hand Easter Dress

"Me something? Me something?"

John, three years old at the time, hopped around excitedly as Doris and I dragged the big cardboard box over near the window. The two ladies from the church, who'd delivered the box to us, had just left our house.

Mother pulled a little jacket out and held it up to John. "Here's something for you, John. I'll take up the sleeves a little and it'll fit you just fine."

Charitable ladies like the two who'd just left our house collected outgrown and discarded clothing around the community. They brought the garments to families like mine with many kids. Mother, skilled with a needle and thread, made alterations to them so our clothes always fitted us and I never felt especially bad that they had originally belonged to someone else.

She was trying to get John's waving arms into the too-long sleeves of the jacket as I stuck my hand into the box and dug around. My fingers encountered something soft and smooth. I'd never felt anything like it. I eased it out of the pile of rough denim and heavy cotton, afraid I'd tear it. I noticed a nice smell as I brought the softness to the light. It was a beautiful pink dress, could it possibly fit me? I hugged it close. It had to fit, oh, Lord, please let it fit.

Mother looked up from measuring how much she would have to hem up the sleeves of John's jacket. "Well, you found something, didn't you, Sylvie? Just about your size, too."

I couldn't believe it. This dress was different from the usual cast-off though still serviceable garments that we usually found in these boxes.

Daddy worked hard as a sharecropper on farms in the county. Sometimes he got a job at a sawmill or a cotton mill. But even then he was barely able to provide food and a roof over our heads for Mother and us five children. There was never any money for new store-bought clothes.

Times were hard in rural Georgia then, especially for a man who had only a fifth-grade education like Daddy. He and Mother, both from large families, had married very young. The arrival of Doris, two years my senior, was the beginning of their own sizable family. Placid nine month old Jack was the baby right now. The next year would see the birth of my third brother, Ray. Later two other sisters, Janis and Sonja, would join the family.

My fingers caressed the gauzy texture of the dress and traced the shimmery design woven into it.

"Let me see! I want a dress, too." Tiny Margaret, two years younger than me, reached to grab my precious dress.

"No, don't touch it. It's mine. Mother said so." I pushed her away and she sat down with a thump on the bare wooden floor. Her face puckered up and she let out a yell. But I was absorbed in my treasure.

In all my seven years I'd never had a brand-new dress. It couldn't be new, but this one looked hardly worn. Why had somebody given it away? Would the ladies come back to get it, saying it had been put in the box by mistake? I nearly jumped up and ran to the door to see.

At school I'd heard a couple of the girls from more prosperous families talk about getting new Easter outfits. The pretty pink dress would be my Easter dress.

Next day I just had to tell someone about my new dress. I heard two girls talking about their new Easter clothes and I had my chance.

"I have a new dress for Easter, too. I'm wearing it tomorrow."

"I bet you don't. You don't wear your Easter clothes to school until after Easter Sunday."

Frannie's (not her real name) young voice was filled with scorn. But she'd see when I wore my pink dress tomorrow. Just thinking about it made me feel warm and glad inside.

Frannie's family owned two farms and a country store, so she always had nice clothes to wear. But most of the kids at school came from families about like mine so we paid little attention to her airs.

Next morning I crammed the last of my buttered biscuit in my mouth before running to carefully pull the pretty pink dress over my head. It settled softly around me and I asked Doris to tie the sash in back. I felt so rich.

I fairly floated along the dirt road beside Doris as we walked to school. The bell was ringing for the start of classes when we arrived so I didn't get to show off my finery. I saw Frannie looking at me with a funny expression though as we trooped inside the building.

The morning dragged on forever it seemed as the teacher called the roll and we had reading class. Finally it was time for recess and everyone raced outside to play.

I looked around for Frannie and saw her over near the swings with her friend, Diane. They had their heads together, whispering. Frannie pointed toward me and they giggled. I started walking over to them. As I passed by the see-saw a girl named Missy called out to me.

"Frannie said it was her Easter dress last year!" Her mocking words echoed in my ears and I felt like I'd been drenched in ice-cold water. I stopped and looked from Missy to Frannie and her friend. Were they snickering and making fun of me and my pretty dress?

The playground in front of me blurred as my eyes filled with tears. Frannie and Diane walked toward me, voices and giggles getting louder. I looked down at the dress I wore. It had not changed. It was still the loveliest dress I had ever owned.

Suddenly an idea came to me. I didn't remember right then that it was in the Bible.* Some Children's Sunday School lesson had evidently found root in my heart. I blinked back my tears and turned to face their taunts.

"Frannie! Missy just told me that this was your dress. Thank you so much for giving it to me. I'll take good care of it."

Frannie stopped, the jeering smile wiped from her face at my words of gratitude. She muttered something that might have been "OK" and ran inside with Diane.

The lesson I learned that day has stayed with me. No matter how they come, I can receive God's blessings joyfully. And the key to that joy is my own attitude.

That grade-school episode may be the root of one of my favorite activities. I love yard sales and search out "Nearly New" consignment shops. Often I find that "pre-owned classic" that suits me better than a crisp new department store purchase. Plus being easier on my pocketbook.

*Luke 6:28

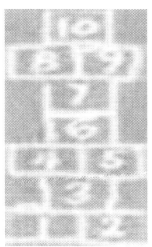

Hop scotch game
markings

Let the Games Begin

Seldom did we prefer being indoors when golden sunshine beckoned. Mother encouraged us to run and play outside, rather than hang around underfoot while she did her many chores. Sometimes if the current baby had reached the crawling/walking stage she would assign one of us to watch to see that he or she did not wander off. The great outdoors was our play room. Walking barefoot in the hot sand in the summer, squishing red mud through our toes when it rained. The lovely feel of the soft new grass in spring when we could take off our shoes and go barefoot, usually the first of May.

My playhouse had lines of rocks for the walls. I would find large flat rocks for my table and stove. Smaller rocks outlined a bed. Colorful broken pieces of glass served as dishes and decorative items. These were parts of broken dishes, some with pretty designs, crockery, pieces of broken vases. I collected this broken glass as my 'treasures'.

I kept them in a white enamel bucket, rusty around the edges, and took it with me whenever we moved. I was always anxious as to whether Daddy would let me take the bucket with us. The pickup trucks that he usually borrowed to move our belongings were hardly ever very big, and he might tell me there wasn't room. I usually managed to find some small space in which to push my precious bucket.

Wild 'poke salad' (pokeweed) grew along the fences at the big barn of Johnny's big house. The tall green plants bore big red berries in the summer, bursting with dark red juice. We were told this juice was poisonous, which it may have been, but it made great 'ink'. We had very little paper on which to draw or write with this 'ink', but we used old boards as our slates and any other surface we could find, including our own skin. This did not particularly please Mother, but it was not a whipping offense.

School paper was precious and doled out to us on a strict 'need to have' basis. Wasting it was a major infraction. The only paper for drawing and doodling on was the backs of calendar pages as the year passed and each was discarded. We campaigned fiercely over who would get the rare paper each month.

With a stick we drew hopscotch games on the ground. A favorite place was the level sandy front yard of the bigger house that belonged to Uncle Davis. Doris usually won, being older and having longer legs. When cousins came to visit, we played 'Red Rover', which involved one team throwing a ball over the top of the house to another team and they tried to catch it as it rolled off the roof.

Organized games were seldom a part of our school regimen. Nor was school-owned equipment available. Any bat, ball or glove was brought from some student's home and the owner had the option to dictate how the game would be played.

'Dodge Ball' was played at home and school. Two members were chosen to be the throwers. They stood at either end of a prescribed area and threw the ball toward the rest of the children who were stationed between these two. If anyone was hit by the ball, they had to take the place of the one who had thrown the ball.

'Jump Board' was a favorite two player game, but with more chance of getting hurt. Mother discouraged us from playing it, but seldom forbade it. A short piece of board, two or three feet long, was laid over a rock a few inches high. The taller the rock, the higher the board came off the ground, the better player you were. One participant stood on an end of the board and then the other jumped on the opposite end. This catapulted the first player into the air and when he or she descended and landed on the board again, the other player was catapulted into the air. The first one to miss the board and fall was the loser.

We made our own checker boards, using whatever odd piece of cardboard or thin wood could be found and two brands of soft drink bottle caps for playing pieces. Kings and queens were created by stacking two caps.

Moving pictures, movies, existed in the 'forties, for many people. Even for us when we lived near Heflin, in 1943. For whatever reason, Daddy decided to take the family, he and Mother, Doris, Margaret, and myself, to the picture show.

I have no idea what was playing. But when we came out the sky looked strange and threatening, constant lightning, roiling clouds.

The electricity had gone out and the street was dark. We, along with some other people, took refuge in a closed beauty shop nearby which the owner had apparently unlocked. In those days when women got 'permanent waves' put in their hair, it was rolled on big rods which were wired to some kind of electrical machine. Mother tried to keep us curious girls from going near the machines, afraid lightning would run in on them and hurt us. I believe a tornado was sighted in the area, but we finally managed to get home safely. That was my first, and last, movie until we moved to Villa Rica in 1950.

Community pools were non-existent, at least in rural Haralson County in those days. But we found 'swimming holes' on some of the many creeks which ran through the countryside that were deep enough to play in. The following is another bit from my brother, Ray's, website.

The Iron Rail Bridge

The place was a swimming hole we often went to located just upstream from an old iron rail bridge. The bridge spanned over a stream known in

Haralson county as Smith's Creek. Something I had noticed about that old bridge was a badly bent place in the rails on one side. I vaguely remember a story that was told that a school bus had rolled backwards down the grade on one side of the creek and smashed into the bridge railing. To get more detail about the bridge and the swimming hole I asked my older siblings if they remembered 'Smith's Creek'. My oldest sister Doris, the J.E. Maner Family Matriarch, did remember that creek but it was not Smith's creek bridge but another bridge in Haralson county that had the iron rails. She didn't remember the school bus incident in either place. My sister, Sylvia, sent me an E-Mail as follows:

Oh, yes, I have memories of us swimming there. But I don't remember any details about the bridge. Even that it was there actually. A vivid memory is of John falling down on his back under the water, he was very young, three or four, I think. That would have been around the time you were born, so we must have kept going there for several years. Anyway, he didn't get up and I was trying to *get to him. I could see him lying on the bottom, probably only inches from the surface. The water was very clear and only about knee-deep on me as I recall. But it felt like I was trying to wade through molasses! You know how they say it is. Well, it's true. I did get to him, obviously, and pulled him up. He had still made no effort to get up himself. Terrified, I guess.*

We would beg to go swimming there in summer. But Daddy didn't take us too often.

I think about one of the last times we went there, at least, that I went, was when I was fifteen or sixteen. I believe Aunt Jewell or somebody went with us. I can't remember for sure who it was. There are some pictures of it in one of Mother's albums that Doris has. It had changed by then, somebody had put some nice sand down there and the bridge was concrete, I think.

That's about the sum total of my memories of Smith Creek. Feel free to use any or all. I look forward to reading it.   Syl

Actually I believe now that last time I remember going with the family to play in the water was to another creek on Highway 120 in Haralson County. The above and other stories of our family from the perspective of my 'baby' brother, who has now passed the half-century mark, can be found on his extensive personal and Maner family website - http://www.raymaner.com

Sibling Support

On my bedroom wall hangs a dainty, lace-edged pillow. In fancy script it bears the message, "Sisters are forever and I'm so glad you're mine."

It was a small gift from my sister, Doris. When I look at it my thoughts tumble back through the more than fifty years to a school field trip when I was a first grader and Doris was in second grade. She took off her sandals and let me wear them because the sharp gravel hurt my bare feet.

I didn't know it then, but she was aggravated with her little sister acting like a baby. I just felt happy to have a big sister who cared enough for me to let me wear her shoes and brave the painful gravel on her own bare feet.

I have a vivid mental picture of my five year old self, tears streaming down my face, as I tried to keep up with my classmates. My shorter steps as well as the sharp-edged gravel held me back.

I had been eager to start to school. But we lived in Alabama and according to state law I should not have been there. State law was that a child must have his or her sixth birthday before January 1 to begin school in the fall. And my date of my birth is   January 29.

We'd moved to a house in the country near Heflin, Alabama just before school started and Doris had been reluctant to go alone to the new school. Two years younger, I was more outgoing than her so Mother fudged on the school records and enrolled me so that I could be with her.

Learning to read and count was fun and I enjoyed school most of the time. That day though

I wanted with all my heart to be back at home with Mother, little sister Margaret and baby John. Why did we have to leave the cool brick school building with its smooth wood floors dark with oil to walk along this rough gravel road on this unusually warm and sticky September day?

The bright sun sparkled through my tears as I picked my way more and more slowly along the road until I was the very last one in the group. I came to a large rock and plopped down on it. Everybody was ahead of me anyway.

It sounded like fun when the teacher told us we would walk to the second grade teacher's farm, to see the chickens and pigs and goats. We'd lived on a farm, but I'd never seen a goat. But this walk was not fun. I flung away the wilted wildflowers I had picked and looked at my feet. I wiped the smudge of blood from a sharp gravel cut on the side of one dusty foot.

Finally Mrs. Massey, my teacher, noticed how far behind I was and came back to see about me.

"Sylvia, honey, what's wrong?" She asked when she saw my tear-streaked face.

"It hurts my feet and I want my sister." I whined. I was past caring if she did think I was acting like a baby.

"Where are your shoes, dear?"

"I don't have any yet. It's not winter."

Accustomed as we kids were to going barefoot all summer and needing shoes only in winter, my lack of shoes or sandals had not bothered me until this awful field trip. Mrs. Massey understood the situation, a not uncommon one in the rural South in the 'forties.

She took my hand to urge me on. "Well, we have to go on, we'll be left behind. You can see your sister when we get back to school."

"She's up there with her class." I pointed ahead.

"Miss Gray's class? What's your sister's name?"

"Doris Maner." I gulped, as a ray of hope flickered. Maybe Doris and I could go back to the school and wait for the others.

"Bobby." Mrs. Massey called to one of the boys. "Run on ahead and catch up with Miss Gray's class. Ask her to send Doris Maner back here, tell her that her little sister needs her."

"Come, Sylvia, we'll keep walking and meet your sister. You'll feel better then."

She was kind but with the responsibilities for the whole class, she couldn't give all of her attention to my discomfort. I only knew that the sharp gravel bit more cruelly into my feet as she hurried me along.

In a few minutes, as I wiped my eyes with my fist, I saw Doris coming toward us. Relief rushed through me, causing more copious tears to flow.

"What's the matter, Sylvie?" She echoed Mrs. Massey's question.

"The rocks hurt my feet. I want to go home." I wailed.

"Girls, we're way behind the rest. We must hurry." Mrs. Massey's voice was beginning to sound a little annoyed.

"Here, Sylvie, you can wear my shoes."

Doris sat down and took off the sandals she'd been given when a neighbor's child had outgrown them.

"Put them on now. Hurry."

She handed one to me and, sniffling, I slipped my foot into it. Doris moved over and helped me with the other one.

I peeked at her through my bangs. It felt good to have a big sister to take care of me. My tears dried and I stood up, taking a step or two. The sandals were too big for me, but they protected my feet from the tormenting gravel.

We caught up with the other children and soon we all arrived at the farm.

For an hour or so we admired the ducks swimming on the pond and the gentle cows grazing in the pasture. We scrambled around on the moss-covered rocks that surrounded the cold pool of spring water inside the dusky, tree-sheltered spring house where the milk and butter were kept.

After a head count assured the teachers that everyone was present we made the trek back to school, I still in Doris's shoes.

Years later, when I mentioned the episode to Doris, she discounted any special virtue in what she did. She grinned and told me how she felt that day.

"When we got home I was still put out because you'd cried, but you chattered on to Mother about our field trip as though you'd enjoyed the whole thing!"

I smiled back at her. "Maybe so. But what I've never forgotten is that you were willing to give me your shoes and walk barefoot yourself on that awful gravel so I wouldn't have to."

Whether due to the trauma of that field trip or my extreme youth, I have no memory of any of my classmates at Heflin. But I remember clearly the thrill of learning to read. I couldn't wait for school to be over the day I could read all the way through my Dick and Jane reader. I jumped off the bus and ran across the plowed field between our house and the road. I dashed into the house to breathlessly read it to Mother, who was suitably impressed.

In later years, after all my siblings and I had finished high school and left home, I was reminiscing with Mother about school days. She was very intelligent, even though she had only finished fifth grade herself. She talked about how she enjoyed watching and hearing as each of her eight children climbed the educational ladder. She never tired of hearing us recite the same lessons another had learned the year before and helped as much as she could with the reading, writing, and 'rithmetic.

In the spring following my mastery of the first grade readers, we moved back to Georgia and I finished first grade at Draketown. Also second grade. Miss Singleton promoted me for the last three weeks of school to second grade and the following year I went into Miss Lemons's class, third grade.

Before that school year ended we were briefly enrolled at Union School near Corinth community. During that period I experienced the anguish of unfair punishment from both sides via my silence about the clay pig and having an older boy lie about me. Finally, I finished third grade at Oxford, the third school that year, while we lived in the Southern Mill village.

Back in Georgia we made it all the way through fourth grade at Draketown and began fifth. While we attended school at Draketown each time, one of our classmates was a boy who had been stricken with polio as a young child. The family lived just down the road from Uncle Davis's or 'Johnny's big house', depending on the time period, so he was on the bus when we got on it each day. He wore heavy iron braces and was confined to a wheelchair. The husky able-bodied farm boys hoisted Roy on and off the bus each day and into the school building along with his wheelchair.

No one felt sorry for Roy because he wouldn't allow it. He laughed and talked loud and was known to pinch any unwary student who got too close to his chair. Polio was another among the hardships shared by poor families in the 'forties and 'fifties, though even the well-to-do were not immune from the ravages of polio in those days before the Salk vaccine.

Then another move took Doris and me to District Line School for the second time. This was after the Easter dress incident. We lived in a big, old house we called the Biggers house, now demolished. The house was owned by an old couple by that name, set back off the road between Corinth Church and District Line School and Church.

One of our classmates was a girl named Nancy. One day Doris and I let Nancy convince us that we'd get home by the usual time if we walked part of the way with her. She lived somewhere between District Line and Draketown, Spivey Road, maybe, off State Route 113, and she wanted us to walk that far with her. She said we could then take Kirkland Road through the woods, actually the road on which the house once stood where I was born, around to our home. We finally did as she wanted, for whatever reason, knowing we would probably get a whipping when we did get home. Daddy had been driving around looking for us in his old green A-model car when we walked up to the house.

He and Mother were quite worried, fearful we had been kidnaped or killed. Daddy felt that he had to take his belt to us, but it was only a couple of light licks on the legs, probably due to his relief that we were safe.

Both Doris and I were too timid to quarrel with our schoolmates much, but that year some dispute arose between Doris and another girl. They agreed to meet in front of the girl's house and settle it with a fight. I was scared for Doris. Whether more fearful that she would get hurt or of what Mother would do if she found out about it, I don't know. I don't think Mother found out, and the fight turned out rather anticlimactic, neither Doris or the other girl landing any blows.

The only other 'violence' I encountered during our school years was later after we'd moved to Villa Rica. Doris had dropped out and I was a sophomore in high school. Margaret, two of our younger brothers, and myself rode the school bus. A couple of older boys on the bus thought they were a little tough and decided to harass my brothers. Though probably quaking inside, I stood up to them, as mentioned at the end of the chapter on the clay pig episode, and ordered them to leave my brothers alone. Being just rough-hewn country boys, not really mean, they didn't bother us after that.

Unfortunately my brothers did encounter more school violence a few years later. Daddy still worked at Exposition Cotton Mill in Atlanta, where he had started when we moved from 'Johnny's little house' for the last time. After a few years in Villa Rica, and my high school graduation and marriage, the family moved to the city for a couple of years and lived in one of the mill village houses.

John and Jack attended O'Keefe High School and after school one day went with some fellow students to the local YMCA. They were unprepared for the vicious cruelty of city slum kids. A dispute arose as to whose turn it was at the pool table. One of the kids actually bit Jack over much of his body. John's helpless fury knew no bounds as he struggled to escape the ones who held a broken bottle to his throat to prevent him from defending his brother.

I believe Daddy tried to get the authorities to punish the perpetrators of the attack, to no avail. Jack survived with no permanent damage, and Daddy moved the family back to Villa Rica not long after. John quit school before he graduated, though he has gone on to get his GED, and all my other siblings except Janis finished high school at Villa Rica. Janis had to be different. She married while a senior, moved to Carrollton, and was graduated from Carrollton High School.

Almost Our House

Our parents never owned house or land. They moved the family from one rented house to another, sometimes growing cotton and other crops on shares for the owner. This is the story of the tiny frame farmhouse that, in my mind, felt almost like ours since we lived in it three different times by the time I was twelve.

For reasons I'll explain later, we always refer to it as 'Johnny's little house.'

The little house sat on land owned by Aunt Bertha and Uncle Davis. Aunt Bertha was Mother's Aunt, sister to her father, Charlie Rush.

We sharecropped half of the forty acres which adjoined their main farm. Daddy's foster parents, our Mamaw and Papaw, lived in the slightly larger tenant farmhouse nearby and farmed the other twenty acres.

"Is this it, Syl?" My brother, John, asked me as we stood on the site many years later.

"I don't know." I looked around, trying to get the proper perspective. We had detoured past the site of our childhood home while I was in Georgia on my annual visit. Now I wondered why I had agreed to stop. I suppose I hadn't been prepared for the fact that more than thirty years had obliterated every familiar landmark. Trees crowded to the shallow ditch beside the road. They left just enough room for the barbed wire fence marching out of sight to right and left. I seemed to remember being told that a businessman from Atlanta owned the property now.

Doris and I walked barefoot up and down the small hills of what was still yet a narrow country lane, stirring clouds of fine, rosy dust in summer and sinking in slick, red mud in winter. Sometime in the intervening years, the road had been rerouted and leveled.

Now it might be running right through what used to be the front yard. Or even the back yard, where we climbed the half dozen gnarled old apple trees. In that back yard Mother scrubbed overalls and flour sack dresses on a washboard, then boiled them in an iron pot filled with water and lye soap over an open fire.

Certainly nowhere in this forest of tall, straight-trunked, fragrant pines was there a vestige of the tiny peach tree shown in the family snapshot taken when I was a skinny two year old. In that photo, Mother, holding baby Margaret, stood beside Daddy, the scraggly limbs of the peach tree behind them. In front, next to Doris, homemade cotton print dress rounded over my little belly, I squinted into somebody's box camera.

"There must be some sign of that cement porch I helped Daddy build. I'm going over the fence." John seemed intent on finding some remnant of our lives here.

His words stirred up memories of Daddy, young and strong. His shoulders and forearms bulged with muscles, faded blue denim shirt dark with sweat, as he guided a mule-drawn plow through the rocky soil. In addition to the cement porch, he built a sturdy outhouse, and later wired the house for electricity. I thought he could do anything.

"Maybe you ought not. There's a 'no trespass' sign."

He eased over the barbed wire anyway, moving among the trees, eyes glued to the ground. "It was right about here, I think."

"Be careful. There was a well, you know. There might be snakes." My words reminded me of our mother. Full of fear, worn with drudgery, she was continually warning us of possible dangers in everyday life. People do fall in old forgotten wells. She herself narrowly escaped a snake bite.

114

"I found something." John exclaimed. He brought it over to me.

As I examined his find, I noticed that the rock he held actually looked like many small pebbles.

"What is it?"

"Don't you remember? We built the form out of old boards and piled all these little bitty rocks in it. Then we mixed the cement in the wheelbarrow and poured it over."

I smiled at him. "Maybe you should keep it as a memento."

"Nah. I just wanted to see if there was anything left of it."

Thirty year old memory fragments of life in that pint-sized house, like bubbles stirred from the bottom of a pond, roiled through my mind. The photo I remembered from Mother's old album and a small chunk of, possibly, cement embedded with pebbles, were two of the few tangible physical reminders of that life.

I wasn't yet born the first time my family lived there. Doris was the only child. They moved to a house on Kirkland Road, near District Line Methodist Church, and added me to the family. A couple of years later, in another place, my sister, Margaret, was born. When she was about a year old, we moved back into the little house.

This was during the Second World War and all able-bodied men were subject to the draft. When Daddy had to make the overnight trip to Atlanta for the Army physical examination I could barely have been four years old. But I remember Mother sobbed all night. I was too young to understand why.

Poor Mother, she was terrified that he would be drafted, and there was yet another baby on the way. For whatever reason Daddy wasn't drafted. He came back to us and soon we moved from the little house to below Heflin, Alabama, where I would begin school.

When we returned from Alabama, we lived for a while in the larger house, where Mamaw and Papaw had lived, on Uncle Davis's property as well as several other houses in the neighborhood.

Even deep in the country we heard about the war that was going on. John Astor, oldest son of Aunt Bertha and Uncle Davis, served in harm's way, as Uncle Davis had in World War I. Mother would tell us in later years of Uncle Davis joyfully calling to them near the end of the war, "Astor's back home!"

Mother's brother, Uncle Eulas, served in the Navy and Daddy's brother, Uncle Bill, did also and stayed to make it a career, from which he retired. I wrote to Uncle Eulas on board his ship in the Pacific Theatre and he answered, his letters written in several different colors of ink, which I had never seen before.

We had one other semi-contact with the war. One day some men worked on the roads around Haralson County, even the lane which went by our house. Mother kept us inside while they were around. We didn't understand their speech, and she told us they were prisoners-of-war. If they were German, I'm sure our humid Georgia summer was not pleasant for them.

Following John's birth near Heflin, we came back to Georgia for a while, returned to near Oxford, Alabama for another year or so, then Georgia again. I had two more brothers and a third sister, Janis, by the time we moved into the little house for the last time.

It was quite snug - three small rooms in an L-shape. Two rooms on the front, or long side of the L, had doors that opened to the bare dirt yard, and, later, the porch Daddy and John built.

We slept three to a bed, enjoying the shared warmth on winter nights. Hot, sticky nights of summer brought fretful complaints. "Move over, you're making me hotter."

Mother cooked our meals on a big woodburning stove in the kitchen, which formed the short length of the L. About twenty feet of roof extended from the kitchen door, sheltering the back steps and the plank housing of the well.

A bucket tied to a rope and pulley setup was attached to the well housing to draw up the household water. The rope fed through the pulley and wound around the windlass, a round piece of wood, about two feet long and several inches thick, with a turning handle driven in one end. If whoever was drawing up water let go of the handle the full bucket plunged back into the well, rope flying through the pulley, windlass and handle spinning madly. Only a rapid backward leap prevented a painful whack.

Family entertainment, other than games of our own invention, was a battery-powered radio, with its usually homemade wire antenna stuck out the window. Besides Daddy's country music, then called 'hill-billy,' I was introduced to those mothers-of-soap-operas, 'Stella Dallas' and 'Ma Perkins' via that radio, which were daytime shows. In the evening there were the old time radio dramas, 'The Shadow Knows' and 'Sky King.' Any news we heard of the war overseas also came over our small radio or the larger floor model up at Aunt Bertha's house.

While we lived in the little house this final time, one of Mother's cousins married a man named Johnny. Uncle Davis gave them the forty acres, which included the larger house as their residence and the house we lived in, which became 'Johnny's little house.'

They filled their house with nice furniture, including a small refrigerator. For some reason, they rarely stayed in their home though, and were up at her parents' house much of the time. When they told us we could use the ice from their refrigerator when they were not there, it was one small luxury in the midst of our poverty.

Birth and death were part of our lives in the little house. Another baby girl was born early in February of our last year there, delivered at home as we all had been, but she came too early. I overheard the grown-ups whisper the words, "bluc baby," a term used for premature infants then, as their skin was often blue from lack of oxygen. Incubators didn't exist then, to aid tiny undeveloped lungs, and she lived only five days.

The miniature casket stood in our front room, as was the custom then, for a day or so. I touched the cheek of my doll-sized baby sister and the ivory-hard feel of it sent cold shock through me. We huddled in a frigid country church for the funeral, and Mother's grief was deepened because she was too weak to be there.

When Doris and I reached eighth grade, we caught the bus to the county seat, Buchanan, and the consolidated school there. I met a 'town' boy and felt the first stirrings of puppy love. Someone took a snapshot of us with his arm on my shoulder. I didn't dare let Mother see it, she would have had a fit. Then we were freshmen at Buchanan High School. But we were there for only half the term when this final and longest time in 'Johnny's little house' ended.

During that year Daddy began working at a textile mill in Atlanta instead of sharecropping for Uncle Davis. Our financial situation improved somewhat. Doris, now fourteen, even received a watch for Christmas. So we moved again, leaving 'Johnny's little house', apple trees, cement porch, and my childhood behind for good.

Two years later, death touched us again when we lost a baby brother, Robert, at six months. A year after Robert died, another blue-eyed baby sister, Sonja, came along, the last baby in the family.

Doris left school to work in a factory. I finished high school and found my first job. Marriage, motherhood, and a move to another state followed. Two brothers went to war in Viet Nam, but God brought them back to us safely. All but one sibling married also, but several of the unions ended in divorce. To my shock, even our parents were divorced after thirty-seven years and ten children.

When I was in my forties, Daddy died on a cold day in February, only two years after Mother's death. A part of me felt again like that young girl for whom the touch of her baby sister's ivory cheek brought home the reality of death.

On this day my brother and I stood (maybe) on the lane of our childhood and the wind sighed through the pine trees. John still held the chunk of pebbles in his hand, the remaining cement holding them close to each other. I reached for it and thought of my sisters and brothers and their families. The cement that had kept us close was love and the memories we shared, among many others, of life in the little house that once stood here.

"Let's get on to Doris's house. They'll be wondering where we are!" I tossed it back to him and headed for my car.

Notes:

'Persimmon Memories,' one of the preceding chapters, in an edited and much shorter version, appears in the Adams Media print anthology, 'Rocking Chair Reader-Coming Home,' October 2004.

The following essay, 'Scenic Route,' originally appeared in 'Blue Magnolia,' a lovely, short-lived online ezine edited by **bj lowry**, which she no longer publishes. Thanks, bj, for using my essay.

Scenic Route

The red, white, and blue Interstate sign summons me to the on ramp. Another miles-long commute to work on a mundane four-lane highway, gripping the steering wheel of my car lies ahead. This daily repeated trip hardly provides the entertainment of the idle afternoon rides along rural roads I remember as a child of ten or eleven in Georgia. An older cousin and her husband sometimes invited me to go with them on a meandering drive in the country. I went more to savor the rich aroma of the back seat's soft leather upholstery than the resiny smell of the tall green pine trees on either side of the road.

The yards of most of the widely separated country houses we passed boasted beds of glorious flowers edged with rocks of assorted shapes. Zinnias, Mother called them Old Maids, and gladiolas in every hue of the rainbow stood tall over yellow marigolds and the gray of Dusty Miller. Baskets of red and pink begonias were suspended from beams while pots of petunias, solid colored and variegated, graced the outer edges of the porches.

Spring in Georgia always brought the white glow of dogwood blossoms lighting the stands of leafless oaks and scrubwood punctuated with evergreens.

Isn't that a patch of dogwoods at the next exit? There must be fifty to a hundred in the triangle of ground formed by the ramp, highway, and frontal road. Their beauty illuminates the interchange, the massed white blossoms seeming to shimmer with inward light. Harbingers of (almost) spring catch my eye. Prolific Red Bud bushes grace the median and decorate the shoulder, purple blooms crowding their bare limbs. Some branches reach to the sun while others are low to the ground, almost touching the dead grass that as yet shows no sign of green.

Drifting fog brings my attention back to the highway as it dips down to the long double bridge over the murky river. A truck thunders by in the passing lane, several large oddly shaped, canvas-covered objects on the flatbed trailer behind it. The wind of its passage nudges my car sideways and my hands tighten on the steering wheel.

Red tail light gone in an instant, the car ahead of me vanishes into the whiteness filling the river valley from rim to rim. Unwelcome images of a bridge collapsing, dumping cars and drivers over a sudden precipice, from TV news stories pop into my mind, triggered by the disappearing tail lights.

This one hasn't collapsed and I follow the road as it rises and curves to the east on the other side of the bridge. A delicate radiance, soft as light filtered through a delicate silk scarf, pierces the fog. The brightness increases as the road climbs, and then I leave the last smoky tendrils of fog behind and face the rising sun.

From a ridge, the highway becomes twin ribbons of concrete winding through the valleys, seeming to meet and disappear in the distance. I wonder, if I just keep driving, what will I find over the next hill, and the next? The challenge of an 'Authorized vehicles only' sign posted at a crossover brings another youthful memory to mind. A rutted, logging track parted the woods near my home. I thought of exploring the track, but lacked the courage. Instilled by my elders, fears of 'moonshiners' and wild animals stifled the yearning for adventure.

Here stands a small Pentecostal Church, its companion cemetery climbing the hillside behind it. Next in view, white and well kept, is the 'house of many gables', I count ten, more than Hawthorne's famous house.

Nearer the city stands another thicket of trees, expectantly awaiting its new leaf-green, spring garment. Only a couple of weeks ago it was a cotton-candy fairyland. A late season snowfall had left each tree branch and clump of dry grass nestled in pure white softness.

I pull into the parking lot between the railway tracks and my building. A soft breeze touches my cheek and sets the small, red flowers on slender stalks dancing in the sun along the right-of-way.

Delight at my serendipitous discovery wells up. An Interstate highway commute can be just as captivating as the nostalgic memory of a scenic drive in the country.

Columns

This last section consists of five of my columns, *'Ramblin' with Sylvia.'* These columns are archived on my web site, http://www.sylvianickels.com, along with several others. I hope one day to be a syndicated columnist featured in newspapers and magazines. Dream on, you say? Yep, I'm a dreamer, always have been.

Sylvia

Highway to Freedom

" ---'s just another word for nothing left to lose." Are you old enough to fill in the missing word of this plaintive '60's tune? The counterpoint is, "everything to gain," but that wouldn't have fit the mood of the song.

Not long ago, when the alarm jangled in the morning, I reached over to slap it off, grumbling, 'Morning already?' Just like everyone else. Then due to a set of fortuitous circumstances, including the fact that I had been born fifty-five years earlier, I was liberated from the Monday through Friday gig. Freedom!

My company had begun moving many of its operations to another state, including the department in which I worked. My husband was even closer than I to retirement, he wouldn't leave. I didn't want a long distance marriage, so I declined the opportunity to relocate. My twenty years service with the company, together with my age, equaled the magic number of points for early retirement. And, since my entire department was moving, taking my job, I would also receive severance pay.

No matter that my retirement pension was a mere fraction of what it would have been at sixty-five. With a year's severance pay and my bit of retirement, I could stay home and write and have long visits with my grandson in the summer. Freed from the daily grind, scheduling the remaining classes required for my college degree would be easier. There would be time to get more involved in my community, even to clean windows if the mood should strike.

There's an old saying, 'youth is wasted on the young.' I would rewrite it, 'freedom is wasted on the young.' With a few years under your belt, you know a little about what you'd like to do, and (maybe) have the courage to try it.

Freedom, to me, is having the time to examine all of your options, and choose. The time may come when I will want to see just how much clout, if any, that degree gives me in the work arena. But, for now, that highway to freedom I took at fifty-five still looks good.

Visions Create Reality

I did a nostalgia type column last week. I guess you could call it an Old Year retrospective. Like sixty years ago. So maybe I'll try my version of a New Year's piece this week, even though it's a tad late.

I was sorting through some accumulated notes and column ideas before placing them in one of my new filing cabinets. One note was a few words exploring how new things replace the old.

Autos began replacing horses and buggies at the turn of the last century. That was before the 1900's began, for any infants who might be reading this!

Horses and the conveyances they pulled had been around for thousands of years. Consider the audacity of Henry Ford imagining he could improve something so venerably ancient, for the benefit of the common man.

But imagine it he did and his dream became reality. However it was an all or nothing concept. Mr. Ford couldn't just install a gasoline engine in a buggy and hitch a horse alongside to take over if the engine failed. Some of the early auto owners may have wished he could.

Many people thought these 'new-fangled automobiles' would not last. Noisy. Scared the livestock on farms when they roared by at twenty or thirty miles an hour. Caused horses to bolt and lose their riders or the carriages they pulled. Put people out of work, too. Leather harness and whip makers, builders of coaches and carts, horse ranchers and traders.

For good or ill, the contraptions did remain. Became bigger, faster, and now ordinary men zoom around on the earth at speeds unheard of in the past by even kings.

When the Wright brothers took to the air very soon thereafter they encountered the same problem. They couldn't just put wings on a car and leave four wheels attached so if it fell it would just roll on along. Well, planes do have wheels, but of another design. Many did fall before flight for mankind became a practical reality. Neither Ford or the Wright brothers or those who came after gave up on their dreams for the future of transportation. They refused to accept the verdict of naysayers.

You or I may never envision a marvelous invention to benefit all mankind. And anyone with a deeply vested interest in the old is not too likely to embrace the new wholeheartedly. But we all have dreams. Pick one and go for it - all out - or leave it alone. Success does not lie around, waiting to be picked up by just anyone. Move off the beaten path, even just a little way, find your vision, and make it reality.

Up the Ante

I'm not much of a poker player, but I know that 'upping the ante' means adding to the pot, so that the win or loss is greater. This appears to be the way I have approached my creative efforts in life. I listed as many of the creative projects I could think of that I've attempted and completed in my lifetime. Of the fourteen or so, only a couple would have had much impact on my ego had I failed.

I might have wanted to wear a scarf on my head for a while if my hair had turned green after I colored it with henna. Failing to earn my degree after waiting 50 years to try for it would have crushed me. Having stories and articles rejected by an editor can be devastating to a writer.

I didn't really realize the types of creative projects I had attempted, and mostly succeeded in accomplishing, during my life until I started making the list. And I probably missed several, or didn't count some that I thought didn't count as being 'creative'. Among those I can remember:

Leader, Sprint Quality group, UFOS

charter member of a Toastmasters Club

company Speakers Bureau member

short-lived church newsletter editor

designed screened-in back porch (Dave the builder improved on it)

The other creative projects I did earlier in my life were things I wanted to do for me. The paper bead necklaces I created turned out prettier than I expected and this pleased me. The half-dozen or so blown egg Christmas ornaments were lovely. These were small projects, because I had little time in those days since I was taking care of my small daughter, my unwell mother-in-law, and her big house. But being able to complete two creative projects was encouraging. I also taught myself to sew at this time and made a beautiful red satin dress, which I've never worn.

These successes gave me courage to try bigger things when I had more time and more motivation to do so, after we bought our first house. I took ceramic classes with my sister-in-law and made several pieces that delight me, especially my red temple jar and speckled bean pot with painted flower trim.

Later I became interested in alternative energy and built a passive solar heating window unit when we bought a bigger house. It worked, but I really was not too pleased with its appearance outside or inside where it poked through the window. I sewed curtains, planted flower beds, refinished a chest of drawers, wallpapered the bathroom and built a shelf unit for it, laid carpet on our front and back porches and put together a back porch water fountain.

Again, these were projects I chose to attempt, and not a lot was riding on the outcomes of the individual projects. But, I now know, they were building up my courage to attempt something I'd wanted to do since childhood - write. I wrote some small things, entered a few contests, and lost. When I look at some of the things I wrote then, I chuckle. No wonder I lost contests and no one would publish my stuff. But I was learning. I subscribed to Writers Digest and bought some of their books. I got discouraged.

Then I began a program to earn my college degree, a dream almost as old as my writing dream. I put the writing aside for a couple of years and earned the degree. Retired. And began writing again. Perseverance paid off and the next year, a story was accepted for publication in a small circulation magazine. My first acceptance. Another small win of a pot in the poker game of life, concrete, external validation as a writer.

Stone Walls

Personal essays. That's a good way to begin, so the books say, write what you know. Uh oh. If, by some miracle, they're published, my siblings will read them. Perhaps there was therapeutic value for me to write about the red clay pigs Mother sculpted. She discovered them broken and I let my younger sister and brother take the blame. I'll just file it away. Later I find said siblings don't even remember the incident.

I decide to write about happier times. The gravel hurt my feet on a school field trip when I was in first grade and my older sister let me wear her sandals. Mother, a wonderful seamstress, remade the charity box clothes we wore so they fitted us.

Unfortunately, that inspirational magazine I sent them to wasn't interested in "The Sandals" or "The Second-Hand Easter Dress" or even "The

Bridge", which told how I overcame my fear of driving across a narrow bridge. I still think the subjects were great. Maybe, perish the thought, my amateurish writing was the problem.

Southern Living showed some interest in a general nostalgia piece about my southern upbringing, said they'd get back to me. They didn't. I keep the essays in a loose collection, adding one when a memory won't let go of me. Maybe one day I'll write that book on coming of age in the red dirt fields of Georgia. *

I tried straight short stories. But editors didn't care for a young woman who found out she was adopted after her mother's death and searched for her older sister. My sister-in-law loved it though. My story about the fighting sisters must still languish in an editor's forgotten files. I never heard from him/her.

In between, I entered stories in contests, including the Writer's Digest competitions. Not even a 2nd or 3rd place. Would a sane person keep beating her head against a stone wall of rejection?

142

If not for my family's encouragement I might have given up.

That mysterious boarded-up house down the street from my workplace presented an intriguing setting. But the novel bogged down after a few chapters. My great grandmother had to be a strong woman, raising an illegitimate child in that period. She was a good subject. I couldn't get a handle on that one either.

Then I retired, more time to write, I told myself. Back to short stories, mysteries this time. I always loved mysteries. But editors didn't love mine. An idea for a fantasy/s-f story wouldn't let go, so I wrote it and sent it out. Rejections.

A chance for a trip abroad came. On my return home, my husband told me I had to call this editor, she wanted to publish my sf story. I didn't really believe it until several months later when I held the magazine in my hands, a stone wall turned into paper and ink.

*At last!

Tis the Season

Since this week is Christmas, I suppose it behooves a writer to produce a seasonal piece. Just to remind folks. Though anyone who doesn't know it's Christmas must live under a rock unequipped with radio, tv, cell phone, computer, or even Palm Pilot or iPod. Heaven forbid.

Christmas comes each year to remind us that there is hope. We may not always feel it. Sometimes that unrelenting hype about 'tidings of comfort and joy' only makes us feel worse. But there it is. *Emmanuel.* God with us. Come to show us that He understands what we humans endure.

Children see that truth dimly, but sometimes more clearly than adults.

My grasp of the truth was rather fuzzy in my earliest Christmas memory. It was the first time my family lived in Alabama and I would have been about three years old. In fact, my own misty memory is probably enhanced because Mother reminded me of it regularly. We all gathered at Grandma's house on Christmas Eve. She lived nearby, not over the river and through the wood, though. After dark Daddy donned Mother's red jacket and played Santa Claus. We screamed and giggled and pretended to believe it really was Santa. (I probably did!)

My sister, Doris, two years older than me, and a couple of our young aunts, who were near her age, received baby dolls. So did I. But mine was a little tiny plastic job wearing just a diaper. Their dolls were larger and wore dresses and little slip-on shoes. I was not happy and showed it, Mother said, by flinging the unsatisfactory dolly under a bed. But that was the breaks, and I had to play with my doll or not play at all.

I survived that first Christmas disappointment without permanent damage to my psyche. I think. There would be others. Those I survived also. Maybe some Christmas disappointments in a lifetime are a good thing.

When we feel the joy, however fleetingly, we will realize it came with a price. Would any of us send our child, or near and dearest, to Death Row to take the place of even a person who appreciated it? Much less to replace one, or many, who spit on and cursed them?

So turn on the radio or tv and sing along with those well-loved carols we've heard at least a million times. Call someone on the cell phone and wish them a Merry Christmas, or send a cheery holiday greeting email from your computer or Palm Pilot. Soon enough, it will all be over for another year. Though not all over, I hope. We'll need some of this good will to greet those January mail deliveries.

Sylvia's first attempt at writing
picture courtesy of
http://www.raymaner.com

Printed in the United States
84156LV00006B/127-135/A